God Doesn't Love You, Little One

Alysen Dunleavy

Progressive
arents
ress LLC

Progressive Parents Press LLC

www.ProgressiveParentsPressLLC.com

ISBN-10: 0615704735

ISBN-13: 978-0615704739

God doesn't love you, little one.

1

Because he doesn't exist!

People have looked to the sky for God,
but he isn't there.

But in the sky you can see
many splendors of nature – birds in flight,
fluffy white clouds, and the light of the sun
which has traveled millions and millions
of miles to get here!

People have looked in outer space for God,
but he isn't there.

But in outer space there are incredible planets, meteors, and even an International Space Station!

People have looked for God across the far reaches of the Earth, from Denmark to Djibouti, across oceans and continents, but he isn't there.

But the far reaches of Earth do include
many diverse ecosystems, cool species,
and natural wonders!

People have looked for God under
a microscope, but he isn't there.

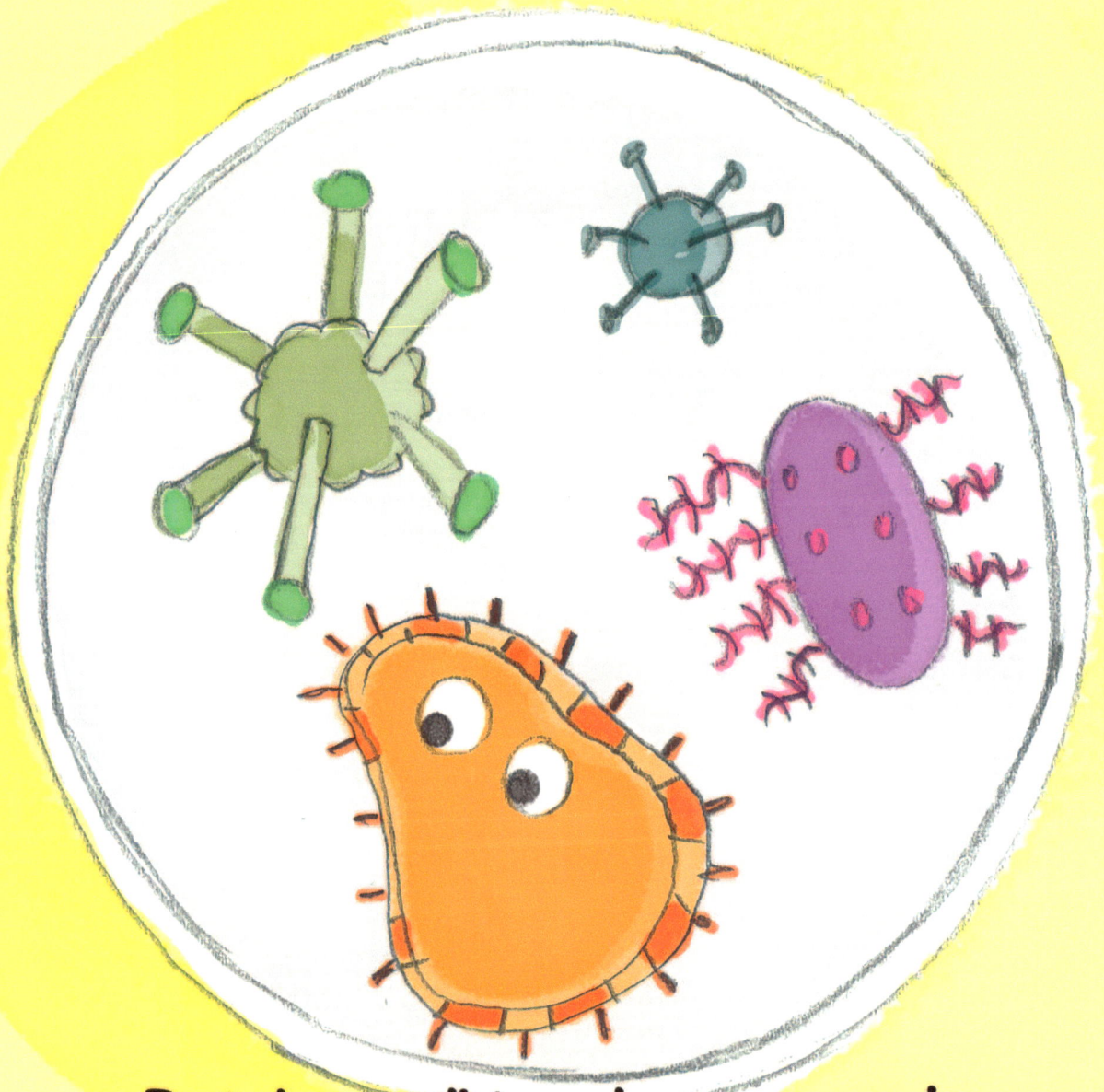

But incredible micro-organisms
like viruses and bacteria can be seen
under a microscope!

Some people claim that God is
in your heart, but he isn't there.

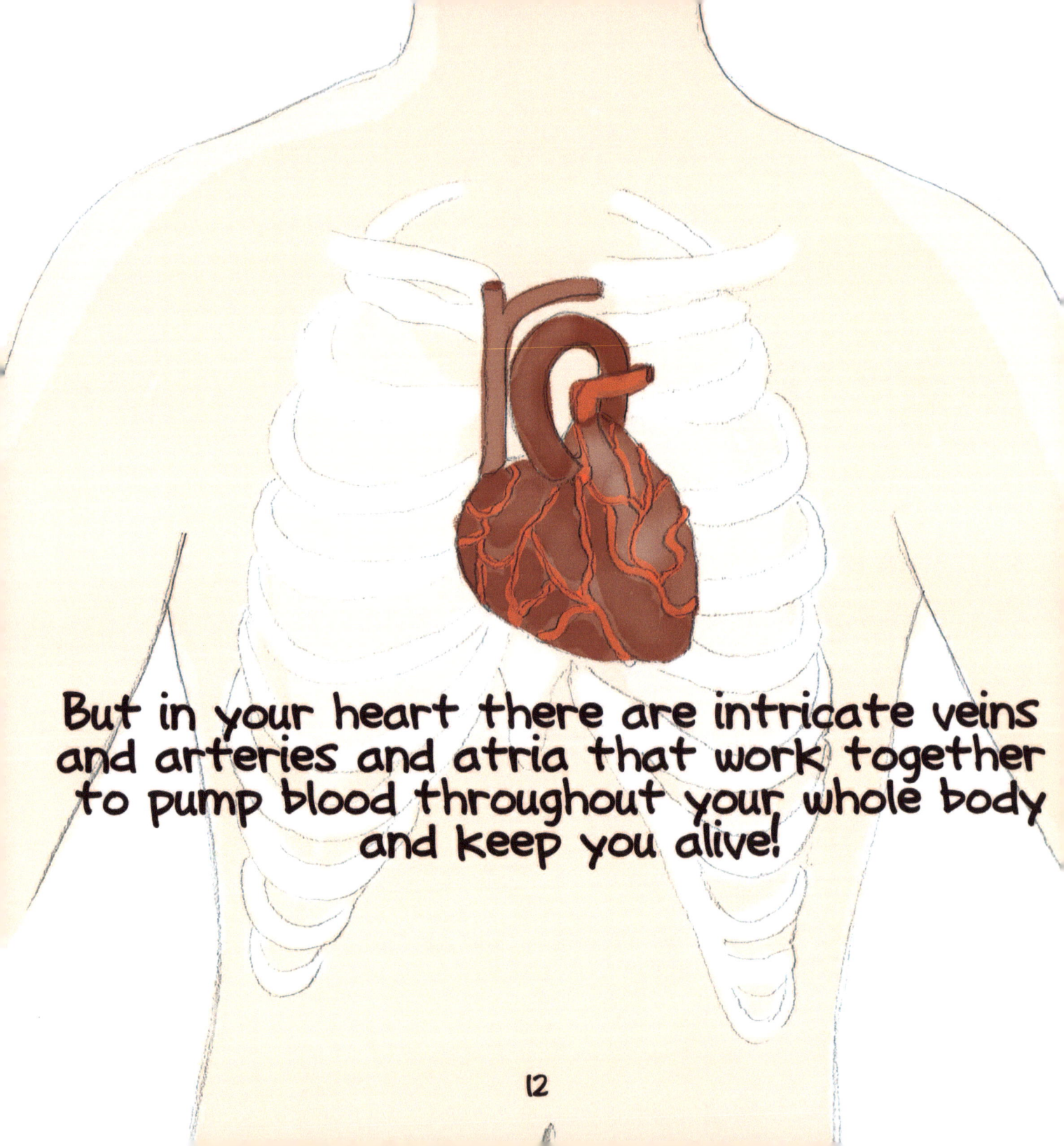

But in your heart there are intricate veins
and arteries and atria that work together
to pump blood throughout your whole body
and keep you alive!

Some people claim that God is in your soul, but he isn't there.

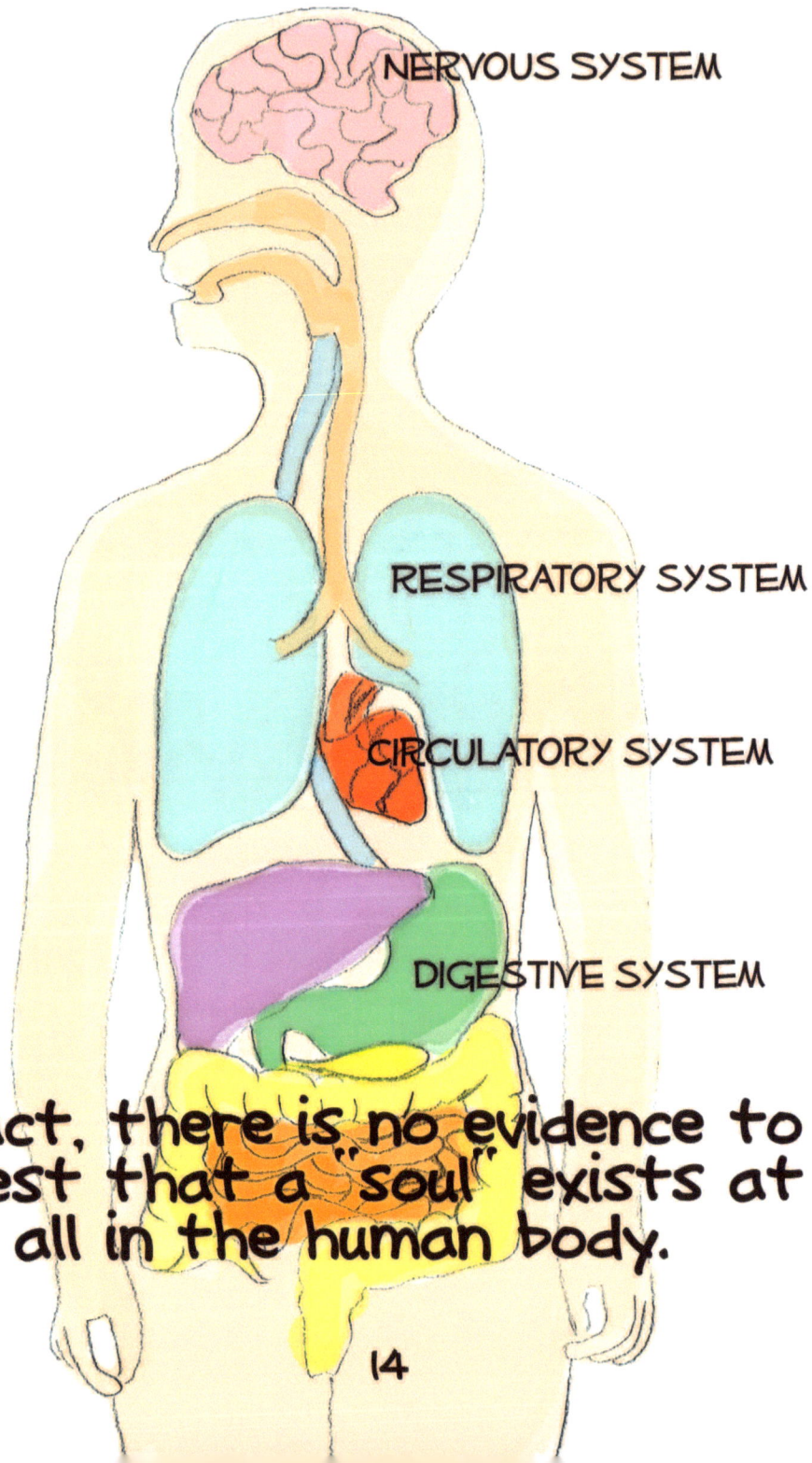

NERVOUS SYSTEM

RESPIRATORY SYSTEM

CIRCULATORY SYSTEM

DIGESTIVE SYSTEM

In fact, there is no evidence to suggest that a "soul" exists at all in the human body.

Some people claim that you will meet
God in heaven after you die.

But there is no heaven.
High powered space telescopes
let astronomers look back
billions of years through
space and time, and there
has never been any sign of heaven.

Some people claim that God must exist because there is no other explanation for certain things that happen in the world, but that's not true.

Advances in science and technology are continually proving that it is nature, not God, that is responsible for things like electricity, weather, and even life.

Some people claim that God must exist because there is no other explanation for the beauty of the world, but that's not true either.

Beautiful things occur naturally without design by a god. And there are many aspects of the world that are not considered beautiful at all, to include regions where life is scarce and temperatures are extreme, such as deserts and tundras.

The truth is that gods exist only in the human imagination and in fiction books, as they have for thousands and thousands of years all around the world.

MYTHOLO[G]
JUDAISM
BUDDHA
HOLY Bible
GREEK GODS

There is less evidence for God than there is for fire-breathing dragons, Pegasus, Big Foot, or the Loch Ness Monster!

So God doesn't love you, little one,
because God doesn't exist.
And that's ok.

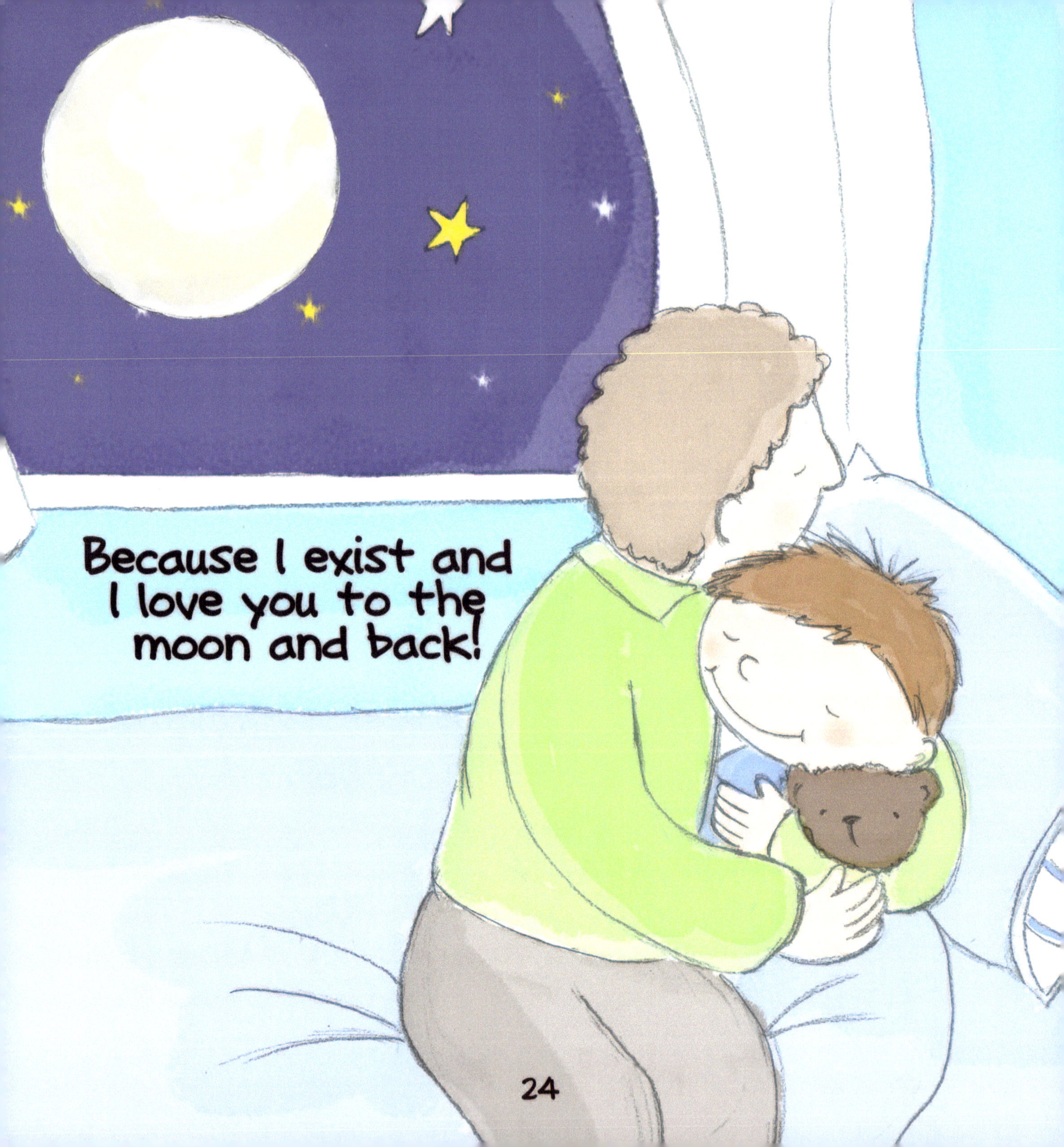

Because I exist and
I love you to the
moon and back!

www.ingramcontent.com/pod-product-compliance
Lightning Source LLC
Chambersburg PA
CBHW042109040426
42448CB00002B/200

9780615704739